She...

Written by Kobi Yamada

Designed by Jenica Wilkie and Steve Potter

COMPENDIUM™
PUBLISHING

live inspired.

ACKNOWLEDGEMENTS

To Heidi, simply my everything.

WITH SPECIAL THANKS TO
Jason Aldrich, Gerry Baird, Jay Baird, Neil Beaton, Josie Bissett, Jan Catey, Doug Cruickshank, Jim Darragh, Jennifer & Matt Ellison, Rob Estes, Michael Flynn & Family, Jennifer Hurwitz, Heidi Jones, Cristal & Brad Olberg, Janet Potter & Family, Diane Roger, Jenica Wilkie, Clarie Yam & Erik Lee, Kobi, Heidi & Shale Yamada, Justi, Tote & Caden Yamada, Robert & Val Yamada, Kaz, Kristin, Kyle & Kendyl Yamada, Tai & Joy Yamada, Anne Zadra, August & Arline Zadra.

CREDITS
Written by Kobi Yamada
Designed by Jenica Wilkie & Steve Potter

She must be something special. She is. Celebrate her.

Celebrate her passion.

She listened
to her heart above
all the other voices.

Celebrate her wisdom.

She pursued big dreams
instead of small realities.

Celebrate her priorities.

She saw every ending as a new beginning.

Celebrate her resiliency.

She discovered her real measurements had nothing to do with numbers or statistics.

Celebrate her self-esteem.

She was kind,
loving and
Patient...
with herself.

Celebrate her tenderness.

She woke up one day and threw away all her excuses.

Celebrate her accountability.

She realized that she was missing a great deal by being sensible.

Celebrate her spirit.

She turned her can'ts into cans, and her dreams into plans.

Celebrate her goals.

She *ignored* people who said it couldn't be done.

Celebrate her independence.

She had a way
of turning
obstacles into
opportunities.

Celebrate her magic.

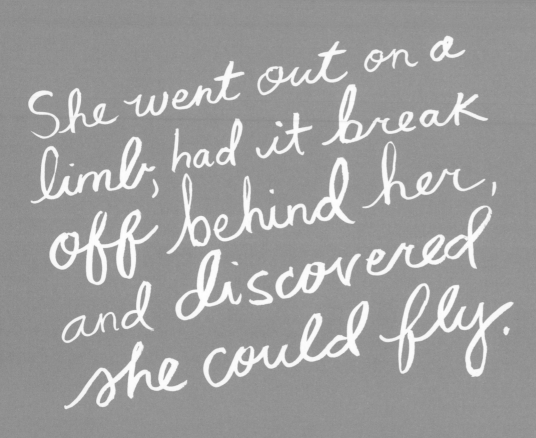

She went out on a
limb, had it break
off behind her,
and discovered
she could fly.

Celebrate her faith.

She discovered that she was the One she'd been waiting for.

Celebrate her self-reliance.

She added so much
beauty to being human.

Celebrate her presence.

She walked in when everyone else walked out.

Celebrate her friendship.

She just had
this way of
brightening
the day.

Celebrate her radiance.

Celebrate her warmth.

She decided
to enjoy more
and endure less.

Celebrate her choices.

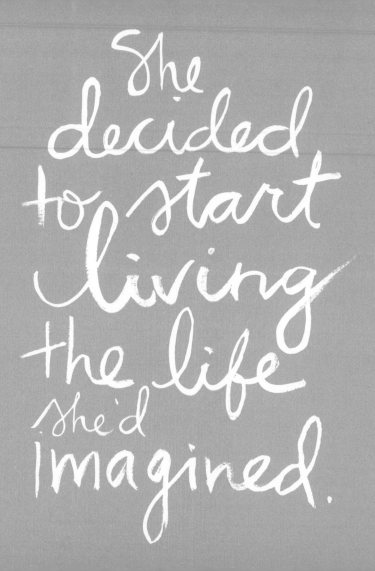

She
decided
to start
living
the life
she'd
imagined.

Celebrate her freedom.

She colored her thoughts with only the brightest hues.

Celebrate her optimism.

She was an artist and her life was her Canvas.

Celebrate her brilliance.

She ran ahead where there were no paths.

Celebrate her bravery.

She crossed borders recklessly, refusing to recognize limits, saying bonjour and buon giorno as though she owned both France and Italy and the day itself.

Celebrate her joie de vivre.

She held her
head high
and looked
the world
straight in
the eye.

Celebrate her strength.

She not only saw
a light at the end
of the tunnel,
she became that
light for others.

Celebrate her compassion.

She designed
a life she loved.

Celebrate her joy.

She took the leap and built her wings on the way down.

Celebrate her daring.

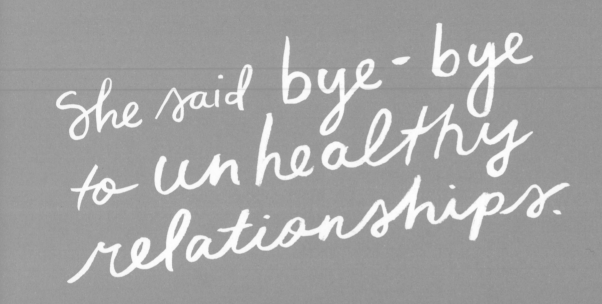

She said bye-bye to unhealthy relationships.

Celebrate her happiness.

She remained
true to herself.

Celebrate her authenticity.

She made
the world
a better place.

Celebrate her.